Library of Lost Lines

Poetry by:

Natalie Ann

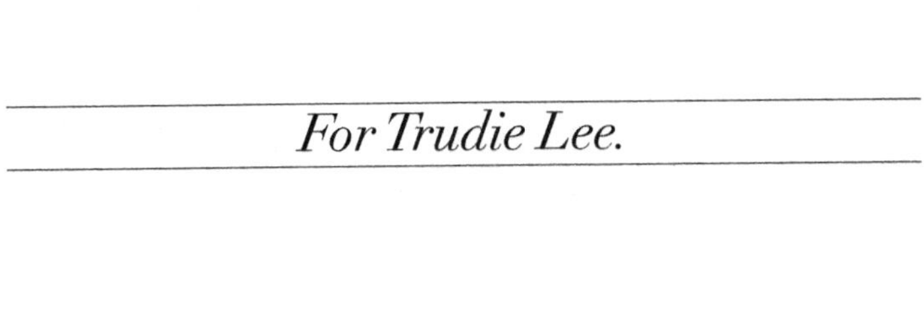

For Trudie Lee.

PART ONE:
HISTORY

How to Speak in Silence

A pair of two
lost in translation –
how do you say love
in our language?

What do we speak
when our bodies meet
and no words
leave our open lips?

Spend the afternoon
with me and learn
how to make love
with the lights on.

Look at me when
you feel like hiding
and I'll teach you
how to trade souls
with the sun.

Midnight

All the quiet, solemn things live in the space on the bed
between us —
crawl to me in the dark, rest your weary lungs on my open
chest.

As the clock strikes midnight, you turn into a ghost — now,
we are the same —
we haunt all our favorite places, fly to occupy empty spaces.

Is your affection a blessing? Or am I cursed?
Fold me in half and feast on my soul — winter-ripened fruit —
I am not sweet but perhaps I can be for you.

The Oracle

This could be fate,
but surely it could still be
a mistake.

Hold me in your arms
and I will decide
to have you either way.

If You Find Yourself Freezing

When I finally caught up to love,
she seemed to be waiting for me.

She carried a coat in her arms
and though she shivered, she passed it onto me.

As I slipped her gift over my shoulders,
I realized why it had taken me so long to find her —

For years I'd kept myself warm when I should have shivered.

Labyrinth

Find me where
I wait for you
in the dark, please.

The walls around me
are a cage I have
grown comfortable in,
a maze I entered willingly
but somehow got lost in.

Am I lost?
Or am I just too scared
to leave?

I run, like always,
but this time I
have someone to run
towards.

I never knew how much
it hurt to leave you until
I no longer had to.

Afterlife

Forever is not a long enough time
to be by your side.

What is beyond forever?

What is longer than our promised eternity?

Swim through time like a river and
wait for me in whatever darkness we will occupy.

Woman

With lavender-scented skin and raspberry lips,
you are a fairy story I heard and forgot the ending to.
I do not trust you, not yet, but I look into your eyes —
something heavenly sighs — and I see myself beside you,
predetermined.
Destiny breathes alongside me as I take your fingers in mine
and I succumb to whatever cruel trick the gods are playing
on me tonight.

Seraph

Angel with a past
and a smile sweet
like death,
you open your mouth
and tell me lies
I want to believe in.

This is church,
I think,
this what I yearned for
as a child.

I have not felt this
form of safety since then —
seven, sitting in a pew,
singing words I didn't understand
and pretending to be good.

Ten Years From Now

Do not be afraid of the future.
For it is not the same kind
of darkness, my dear, as
our afraid masses like to imagine it as.

It is not an expectation,
a noose around the neck
of your childhood dreams.

Let your steps be steps
instead of wishing they were miles.

You will understand, of course,
when you are older and
you find your second youth,
that death is not the enemy.

Instead, it is the only promised companion
that will accompany you home.

This Is My Wish
For You

That somehow, you will find peace
in this world at war —

That you will be comforted
by someone when the walls come down.

A Poet

Like a bear,
I sleep all winter.

I crawl out of
my cave as
the sun thaws
the weeds.

Did you miss me
while I was away?

I dreamt of you
those long months –
I spoke to you
though my mouth
was shut.

Serpentine Soul

You belong in velvet, wearing rings of emerald and a crown
of gold.
You are what they write songs about, poetry of old.
You are dangerous, cursed, beautiful,
and when I touch you I touch history to come.
You sit and suddenly the forest floor becomes a throne.
You pull me in and church is just a building,
just walls and a roof.
Perhaps I am a prisoner,
maybe your hands around my wrists are chains.
But I am weak — you know this —
and I never minded losing to you if it meant you'd stay.

Paradise Found

Meet me where the clouds kiss the hills.

This land knows you as well as I do,
covers your tracks like a lover
wipes lipstick off a cheek.

Let's just stay here, stay.
Let's decay here, let's give our bodies to the bees,
love dripping off of our souls like honey as they head
toward the sun.

I love you, I tell you and the wind carries the words your way.

You reach out, miles away, and your fingers brush my face.

In Pompeii, an Embrace

It must have been a sudden thing,
the shaking of the earth
beneath suntanned feet.
Someone must have looked up and saw
that instead of the sun, the sky held smoke.
The ash must have tasted
like the realization that the gods
were truly, forever dead –
there would be no saving this time,
no war for the immortals to take sides
for there were not any heroes spared, were there?
Underneath the newly formed rock,
a man finds another and takes his hand.

They will unearth you thousands of years later
and find you curled into one another.
All of the artists will call you lovers and
the historians will claim you as
two strangers, afraid, clinging to the
last piece of humanity you could find
before the earth covered you with
the heaviest blanket and
the darkness met you.

Star-lover

In the middle of
the night,
I tip my head back
and the sky falls down
just to hold me.

*You know you are some sad creature
when you wish for rain in March.*

Bacchae

Honeysuckle mouth and myth in your eyes —
what ancient thing do you want to do tonight?
Let your hair down and dance with me on the soil
over the bones of our forgotten heroes,
their stories told in tongues too old for us to recognize.

When you look at me, I am other.
I become what they sing about in pubs after the lights go
dark, after drink wets lips.
I become what only the drunk, in the dark,
are brave enough to remember.

You hold my gaze across the room, then hold a cup to your
lips.

What Could Have Been

Explore with me
the ruins of what
used to be
something great.

Turn east, you said,
toward the sun.
Feel the warmth
on your Roman nose.

The city is cold,
not just in winter,
and everything
tastes like terror.

This kind of terror
is too timid to show
its face until you
take your last step.

You tell yourself
that sometimes,
falling still feels
like flying.

Prometheus Complex

You take it from me
and give it right back –
fast enough, beautifully done,
wrapped in promises and
tied with my tongue.

You like to remind me
that you made me,
that you fought for this.

But when the world
burned down with the fire
you placed in my hands –
that cursed gift –
the ash that filled my mouth
tasted of your kiss.

Honeymoon

Beachside suntanned skin
and her whisper smells of gin
when she says come here.

See the ocean rise
between a lover's thighs
this is paradise.

Curious

The wondering is what catches you.
It swallows you in spite of your cry for peace.

It says to you, slow as cancer, that this
is what happens when contentment expires—
this is what happens when you have
a full pantry but starve for what you suppose
you lack.

This is what freedom feels like after it's left to
sit in the sun for a little while – like choice.

The thing about humans and choices
is that they always seem to choose wrong.

Wish

Heaven waits
and I say
I will join you,
we will become one.

You are the sun
and I am Icarus.

I was always
doomed to drown.

I just wanted to
reach you and

I just wanted to
feel the wind on
my face.

Good Grief

Child of the moon,
sister of the sun,
do you feel at home
in our decaying skies?

If you stay out
long enough,
if you learn to come
home at sunrise,
you will know
our secret histories —
humanity's bones buried
beneath the
new shopping mall.

Are we safe here? Are you?

Sit beside me
and watch the wind.

Have you seen colors like these?

The oceans are full
of oil but
they look so pretty
as the sun sets over
the waves.

Purple - black sea, we sing,
wash me clean,
filth me up and
set me free.

The Traveler

Red cheeks and nowhere to be,
will you let me borrow
the rest of your evening?

Let's kiss just to kiss,
a hand on your hip
as I bring you closer to me.

I'll press an ear to your chest
to hear your heartbeat like the ocean.

The world lives inside you and
oh, how I long to travel the lengths of it
before we both return home.

The Lighthouse Keeper's Lament

Let me show you what it means to be human,
what it means to be born this close to the sea.
Madness isn't madness
if you disguise it as artistry.

Muse

Blush for me, baby,
as you stare toward the sun.

Spring melts Winter away,
causing the pink in your cheeks.

I want you here with me
with my words and
a hair in your hair
to keep you here,
tethered to me.

Wisteria soul, don't leave me.
Stay, let your hair move with
the breeze of winter's last breath.

Somewhere, a bird sings
and you press yourself
closer to me.

As dusk settles over the trees,
the poetry in me stirs from sleep and,
like a moth to a porch light, flies.

Antichrist

There's a star tattooed on your sternum
as though you knew I needed something to wish to
when I'm feeling particularly hopeful.
Can I make you something to believe in?

You and your devil grin, your promises are something
even I can't pretend to hear obligation in,
but they give me a reason to love you regardless of
whether I'm meaning to.

Wild

I want to swallow the storm
hovering close to the hills.
I grew up watching the sky darken,
waiting to be tall enough to
drink the clouds –
I spent all my afternoons with my chin to the sky,
tasting the water that had once belonged
somewhere else and feeling,
as I always did then,
like I was a thing as strange as
rain in summer.

Faith

Pretty little thing,
homegrown and fearful
of leaving —

Open the Earth like
an orange and live
among the seeds –
the rest of the world
exists outside you, waiting
for your return, hoping.

Oh, hope.
Where does it go?

There it was, once,
plentiful as rabbits
living among the weeds,
but there are no creatures here,
only concrete.

Everything is a fairytale
when you don't know
what to believe.

Forever

Lover without anything left to love,
come home. Eternally rest
here, where time passes slowly
and the sunsets last.
Find me in that
otherworldly orange light
and eat me whole,
a sacrifice devoured.

I want to hold you
but I can't remember how.
So I will sit on the graves
of what we left behind
and I will watch you from afar
as you live a life built for
the both of us without me

Shadowed

A black corner of the room beckons.

It is an invitation to the darkest side of me
I know how to acknowledge without
falling into the trap I've laid out for myself.

I spent many years chasing the light I once loved
only to realize how satisfied I seemed to be
when I succumbed to the dark.

It was never something to fear – not really –
for all those years I stared at the dark shadows,
fearing the day they would finally take me,
they were holding me all along.

Homemaker

Nightshade eyes
made by deadly design
call your lover and
tell him you are mine
for the night.

Death and Desire

Leave us, I whispered,
but the shadow at your
shoulder grew darker.

I had forgotten
that I am not the
only thing that waits for you.

Run, quickly.

Run before the rest of us find you.

Instinct

Pink knees and an itch to please,
which level of hell did you escape
to find yourself here, kneeling
in place of another.

Like Eve,
I am desperate to know the things
I do not have words to explain.

Like Eve,
there is something inside of me
which screams *take*.

Finding You in
Mythos, Again

Adonis kept me close but
his beauty kept me distant

It's hard to love a god
when you crave coexistence

What is a god, I found,
but a better version of you?

I knew he would leave
but I never expected you to.

Salvation

What frightening thing
did you see
when you stumbled through
the dark for me?

You, with your wide-eyed stare
and thistle in your hair, come
closer.

I wanted to be good, oh
how I tried.
I wished to be evil, even,
so that I'd have nothing left to hide.

Can I be both? Can it be true?

Can I exist merely as myself when I am with you?

Medusa's Lover

I was not brilliant but I understood —
how lonely it must be to never be seen
or, though you shouted, heard.

Here, let me touch you with hands
that will stay flesh — a warm touch on
your cheek and through your serpentine
hair, a caress.

Take me as I am — let us sail the
boundless sea of their curiosity
until we become as famous as the rest
of the monstrous characters of their
selective history.

How beautiful I would find you if
only these eyes could see.

An Angel of My Own

Though you were of broken wing,
you carried me.

What love – what love.

Ishtar

Babylon-brought baby,
older than God, than time,
what a muse you are
what a tune they've sung
with your name on their
dried tongues.

My desert-dream of a woman,
you say you do not remember
the time we spent together
but you touch me like you've
learned where it is I like to
be touched —

You and your marbled eyes,
sweet like liquor tonight,
bring me what you have left to give —
let us chase the poets with
a song stronger than whatever
they can think to write —

Love me, love me,
if only for the night
for the stars shine so much brighter
when you stand beneath them
and how I love to see them shine.

A Rainbow is a Promise

At first, were they grateful for
the rain?

Did they watch with
wonder as their children
ran amongst the fields
with mud-caked ankles and
a vision of a greener spring?

To all those who were not Noah,
to all the animals that watched
two of their kin board
that strange boat free of any kind of sea

I will never know you as your God did
and yet still, I am sorry.

Eternity

You are a god in a
leather jacket –
something that doesn't
feel the cold on your skin
and yet you shiver anyway
to try to remember
what it felt like to
be so breakable –
fragile enough to freeze.

The worst thing about
immortality, you tell me,
is that you never know
what will be the last time.

You look at me like
I am dying and you
fuck me like I'll live
forever and when you
leave just as it turns
morning, your smile
brings sunrise –
an immortal's silent goodbye.

Darkened Daylight

There's but one hundred feet between us.

Here, in the dark, I feel seen.
Here, with you, night is not night,
it's stars and sunshine combined,
and the gods watch us with a grin.

When we are young,
we carry the world
on our shoulders
and we call it love.

You'll get used to it soon, Venus whispers.
Every path looks like a maze until you know
the way through.

Ordained

Pray for me
as you fall asleep —

Send my name
to the sky,
wait for that eternal reply,
and think of me
as you dream.

I'll meet you in the
in-between,
to kiss your perfect lips as we
listen to our sins.

Girlhood

-95-

It surprised me, the pain.
It felt misplaced here,
present in one of the moments
I most longed for.

I had forgotten what I meant
to be a woman –
to want something
and to get it,
but not without hurting.

MODERNITY

Two Pairs of
Ink-stained Hands

Press me to the page,
pen to parchment.
Immortalize me in a few
pieces of prose –
romance, romance, romance
isn't as dead as you'd
like it to be.

Can I be yours for the rest of your life?

Place me on your wrist and
I'll tell you the time –
time for you and I to
find the things left for us to find.

With your fingers in mine,
write me into whatever love story
you want to tell me tonight.

Magicked

You and your theories —
do you rest when you sleep
or are you running even
as you dream?

You do not have to hide here,
secret sorcerer, not with me.
You can wish all you'd like,
can wish for the future
you hope to see.

A Trip to New York City

I wanted you so desperately —
I was so in love with you that
I started seeing you in
all the empty seats on the subway.

There you were as an eighty-year-old
woman, knitting a scarf in your favorite color
— midnight blue — and there you were as
an angry boy, scowling as he listened to
a CD of all your best songs.

I heard you on the radio — the real you —
and I smiled as I slipped lower where I
sat against the cracked leather of the backseat
of my taxi.

It felt as though I was the only person in the
world as your song played through the
speakers of a car that didn't belong to me.

Isn't it funny what love can do to you?

Who I'd Like to Be at Seventy

If I could be anything, I'd be kind.

Kind to myself, maybe, but
kinder still to those who hate me.

I wish to be as soft and tender as
an April sunrise.

I want to be slow to anger as a
work-worn body from bed on a Sunday.

I wish, I want
to be someone whose lips are not
stained with the name of another.

If I could be anything, I'd be kind.

To The Girl I Left Behind

I saw something and it
made me think of you.

There was no longing to be found
as I recounted those years. No, I just...
I remembered you. Suddenly, I was
myself at seventeen.

I felt the weight of what was to come
above my heart, nestled into my chest
and I recalled your hair – the way it
looked like night as it caught the sun. We
were all contradictions back then, torn
between the versions of ourselves we'd grow
to be and the shells of our girlhood, glistening
against the sands of time.

Isn't it strange the way we knew each other
so deeply at sixteen only to be strangers
at twenty-six? Still, I think of you. I do.

Heaven-Seeker

Cosmos-watcher,
what is it you see in the stars?
Here, you say,
the moon,
a satellite.

I find your knowledge strange
in the absolute best way
because I am afraid of
the things I do not understand
but you —
you watch the night sky and
revel in what you will never know.

How wonderful.

Natural Affection

I speak to the trees
in the same tone
the lovers on my television screen
speak to one another.
Are we lovers,
the world and I?
For I have
never been held
the way the water
holds me each
summer evening
when I've decided
that a walk
to the lake and
a swim will suffice.

Desperado

The red string of fate
looks different where
it stretches between us,
mottled and bruised,
purpled because I asked
you to —
does fate take offense
if you leave her waiting?

Ah, regardless,
leave me here
until I miss you and
don't come back
until I beg you to.

Beast

In my dreams,
I am some
mythic, untouchable thing
and when I wake,
there are rubies
behind my teeth.

Those nights,
I am something else
entirely – too far
removed from humanity
to feel any kind
of remorse as I
burn villages to
ash and bury
myself beneath the
embers to feel warmth
against my skin-turned-scale.

Then, as dawn
greets me and
the cat demands
breakfast, I am
woman again,
and I feel
so *sorry*.

I want to move
the mountains

so that I can
bring the forest to you
you've spent long
enough on the sand

rest here,
where the rivers flow over rock
and when the winds blow,
it will remind you of home

but you will
be here, with me

Curator

When you press your lips to mine,
it's as though I can feel the sun on my face again.
For so long I was a shell of myself,
a portrait left in pencil, unpainted.

How I craved life anew
when you walked in and
saw me not as something unfinished,
but as something that just needed
a little bit more color.

And how I loved you
when you pressed the brush into my hand
instead of your own, content to watch
me as I created myself all over again.

Ulcer

I've not yet grown used to the dark but
when I move to turn on the
brightest light, my fingers still
where they've reached for the switch.

The light is already on, you see,
shining like a man made silver sun
in the middle of my seventies ceiling.

I am afraid, as I tend often to be,
and yet I do not know what it is
I am afraid of.

The sky is one shade lighter than night
and I watch the rest of the day bleed
from behind the clouds and wonder,
as I often tend to do, if I should have followed
in my mother's footsteps.

At least then, I could have held death
in my hands and kissed it quietly.
At least then, I could look illness in
its easily recognized eye.

But I am not like my mother.

So, instead,
I imagine and
I imagine.

My fingers shake as they hold the pen
but it is all they ever learned how to do.

Only You

Let's make music with our sleepless hearts
and restless hands – our bodies are the band,
playing softly as we sing to one another.
Words are so sweet when they are sung
so we sing the things we have otherwise
kept quiet.

We learned from infancy to be
quiet, listening things,
but here, why don't you be loud with me?
Here, ask me a question with only your eyes –
ask me to kill you with a touch only
to bring you back to life.

You sat on your hands at the museum to
starve off the temptation to touch
like a good little boy but now,
since we've grown, you've learned the truth –
the best way to love art is to consume, consume.

Put your hands on me – feel me while I create
something new – kiss me while I write something
else about you. Are you tired of it, endless muse?
Settle among my thoughts again and I will wrestle
you into something you like enough to forgive me again.

Visitation

Are you wild like me?
Feel your breath leave your lips slowly.
Do you beg for it?
Are you afraid of it?
Leave your clothes at the edge of my coffin
and show me what I've missed.
How have we been together all this time
and not been together like this?
Every touch is a gift,
blessings in every kiss.

Angel, don't leave my side.
I don't want to go back into the dark –
I don't want to go back home tonight.

December

I am your winter girl
and I love the way
you shiver against me.

The breath you take
is a hurried, visible thing
as you clutch your frozen
hand in mine.

You tell me you don't know
how I can stand the snow but
among the white-tipped branches
and snow-trodden streams,
I feel at peace.

Here, I am not the coldest thing.

To Fit in Your Palm

These days, I find myself
wishing I was a screen so that
I could have your hands on me.

Nighthawk

In the midnight air, those bright lights
beckoned me with some old-fashioned
sort of safety.

I found myself a diner with unwashed tables, sticky menus,
glass-bottled ketchup, and over crackly speakers,
the radio.

Here, I am helped by a waitress that has
worked her whole life behind that red-coated
counter.

She pours me a cup of coffee with a genuine smile,
the lipstick caked in the cracks of her lips
a faded plum,
and finally, I may exhale.

I feel safer, more at home here,
surrounded by fellow security-seeking strangers, than
I have since I slept in my mother's house.

I can be anything I want to be here,
so I choose to be no one –
just a woman, alone in the corner booth,
shrugging off a plaid coat.

*"It seems love died with poetry. /
Would you like to resurrect them with me?*

Vacant

Empty space and light-washed walls —
somewhere, the sound of the sea.
Do you remember?
It's so easy to forget, you said,
and I couldn't think of a clever reply
so I said nothing.

In my studio, my art doesn't know I'm an artist.
To the paintings on the walls, I am just someone
who knows when it's time to turn the lights off.

As the easel stands alone,
a soldier coming home,
I think to myself that I
should have asked you to stay.

I should have asked you to stay.

Three.

Remember when we could light the sky on fire
with a single match?
When the trees looked like something to climb
rather than hang from?
Sometimes I'd do anything to go back to those
long afternoons – beige carpet and braided hair –
where we'd say *I love you* through grinning teeth
and eat our worries away at dinnertime.

Love in Modernity

You need a home,
I need someone to come home to.
You know it all,
I've got some learning to do.
Tell me all your secrets
and I'll show you where I hide,
peel the lies back layer by layer
until we're naked tonight.

I don't know where this is going
but I'm here for the ride –
roll the windows down
and put your hand on my thigh.
Would you believe me if I tell you
I've been waiting for this moment
all my fucking life?

God can keep heaven if
I can have you for the night.

Vows

I will hold you when the lights go out.
I am here when you miss the last step
and tumble towards me.
I will stay when it fades into
something other than what
you had always dreamt it to be.

I exist, in part, to color the sky blue for you
when you say you remember it gray.
I will say I taught you to see the angels
and you taught me I could be one of them.

C.

You've always loved small, fragile things.

Since childhood, you adored
the otherwise forgotten, the constantly abandoned.
I can picture your tiny hands holding something
the size of your smallest finger – a fairy, maybe,
made of porcelain.

I watched you with wonder as you fell
for every fairytale –
what would it be like, I wondered,
to be someone that believed in the pretty,
hopeful things?

Do you remember the princess nightgowns
you wore to bed? For years, you
wore them not as some kind of reverence for
the characters printed on a plastic portrait, stitched
in satin, but because you believed you were
worthy of wearing such a pretty, soft thing to bed.

I can't help but wonder when you stopped viewing
yourself as someone deserving of niceties.

I hope, someday, you feel
like a princess again.

Flame, Contained

I have always thought of myself
as something volatile
but you take our fire and
settle it into a hearth, a home.

Perhaps there is a piece of me
that mourns the feeling of
leaving the world ash but
come winter, the tile is warm
beneath my feet and you —
you hold me.

You have learned how to keep me close
without dimming my flame and
we burn bright inside our bedroom
made of white brick.

hungry

Shall we unlearn the urge to starve?
Sitting in the corner of the room,
she traces her fingertips against
a clavicle the fat has grown over.

I imagine crossing the room,
taking her hands in mine.
I know what it's like to
find beauty in bones, I'd tell her.

But I wish your bedroom was a bedroom,
I'd say, instead of a coffin you've put
up posters in and
I wish you could taste the sugar of something
on your lips without wondering where it'll
travel afterward.

There's an app you use to track
what you eat and it reads like
the world's most pathetic poem.
For breakfast you had –
eggs (scrambled, no milk)
      coffee, black (no cream, no sugar)
        a slice of toast (multigrain, no jam)

Your mother taped a poster to the fridge.
It reads
      Are you hungry? Or bored?

But you think you are both. Always, both.

To Keep a Promise

A traveler in search of treasure,
I held you in my hands and waited for you to shine.

I dreamt of you and there you were when I opened my eyes,
my Sunday surprise, tanned from summer with winter on
your mind.

You wait for me while I am away
and then, before I can leave again, you remind me why I'd
like to stay.

The Lover and the Logician

I want you drunk on me –
slurring in the streets,
screaming that you love me
talking about me to any
poor, kind soul that takes pity
and stops to listen.

I want you to invent words
to describe the way my
hair looks as I lean over to
light a candle – as the orange
glow hovers over my lips I want
you to turn your one-lined promises
into Shakespearean sonnets.

When they ask about me,
sew your answers into
cashmere and lace.

Convince me you won't
walk out the door and
I'll give you a reason to stay.

Juniper Street

My grandmother loved to eat lemons
and so did I. In my palm, I could
pretend I held the sun or
God's golden heart and against my tongue,
with the sour seeds against my teeth,
I learned to mourn every sweet thing.

My Roaring Twenties

Maybe the billboard on the side of the ten is right.
Probably, the world is ending.

The sun sets at three and I work until eight.
On my drive home, I miss the light, I miss the warmth so
badly that I wish the sun would fall down from where it
hangs, invisible in the night sky, to swallow me.

America bleeds purple but she only knows primary colors so
I sit on my couch and cry on my phone and I think that if
Elon Musk can make it to Mars, I can make it to bed.

It's hard to fall asleep when you're not sure what the world
will be like tomorrow morning,
so I stay up until I'm too tired to care, and then when I fall
asleep I dream that the world is on fire
so that when I wake,
reality feels a little like safety.

To the Youngest

I watch you
work out the
rest of your life
at the dining table
and I remember
what that was
like, being nineteen.

I remember noticing
the way the world
stretched out in
front of me
and wondering whether
I'd ever swim
in the river
I was so afraid
to drown in.

Ah, come here.

Listen.

It was never a river
and I was never
drowning.

Rhapsody

I want you here by eleven.
Please don't be late – I've learned don't like myself much
when you're not here to remind me
of who I really am.

Sometimes I wake at night and my sheets
are warm on your side. Am I losing my mind?
No one told me Cupid traded his arrows
for hunting knives but it's one in the morning
and I'm lying on the carpet, thinking of you
instead of the ache in my chest.

I think that if I had to do it all
over again, I would still choose you.
After all, an addict isn't an addict
unless they have something they
aren't willing to lose.

The Actress

I've always been melodramatic
but it's rooted in truth –
a performer can sing in
front of thousands
and go home to an empty room.

Concierto

Two anxious things sitting in the mezzanine,
startling when the lights come on.
We suffer through the show
and smile at the close,
hoarse voices and sore throats
on the car ride home.

You drive and I watch –
careful, careful, careful.
No music plays through the speakers
so instead, we talk to fill the silence
we don't feel threatened by.

We're two friends that worry
the world away. And
when we're left with the
pieces of each other, only we
seem to know how to
fit them back together.

Library of Lost Lines

Sitting at the table, writing again.

I am creator and lover,
woman and poem
pressed together into something sitting
in front of the rectangular window,
alone.

Like Pygmalion, the sculptor,
fell in love with his stone,
I read what I have written
and I feel at home in the words
I wrote.

It is a strange life,
living for an experience other than
your own.

What a lonely existence,
what a lovely one too –
you don't have to make the mistake
to learn what not to do.

Trudie

If I close my eyes I can see you as you were when you were
still mine,
before the ground took you, before your name became
something written on a stone instead of said from my lips.

Grief is different than I thought it would be –
I think I'm still waiting for you to come home.

I can't seem to pass a window without looking for you
through the glass,
wishing you into all of the empty spaces.
I didn't notice how much of my life you filled until the
whole world started feeling like a long drive and an empty
passenger seat.

How human of me.

Intrusive Thoughts on a Thursday

Breaking down the walls I use to hide,
climbing inside to find the darkest
version of myself tonight.

I've been wondering why I'm like this
for my whole life –
when did I learn I was the only enemy
I'd ever have to fight?

I think I'll set my house on fire
if it means I'll get outside and
when the moonlight hits me,
I won't have anything left to hide.

I don't want to be a winner, baby,
I just don't want to lose.
I asked him is heaven really heaven
if you don't get to choose?

I'm a thief with guilt wrapped
around them like a coat but
I'm the only one from who
I've ever stole.

It's dark where I am now but
still, I run from the light. It's
easier to hide if you're free
from their eyes.

Quick, make a wish,
say it out loud or it
won't come true.

If I'm still alive by thirty
maybe all my wishes
will lead me back to you.

Los Angeles

A Sunday morning, slow to start.
It's too hot – even for summer –
but we lay in our little wasteland
and love each other anyway.

The Addict

Chronically online
and a life half-alive —
fingers curled in your sleep
shoulders bent forward,
misaligned.

What if you knew everything, all at once?
What if you were needed? Wanted?
What if you could be noticed?
What if you were strong on purpose or weak
when you planned to be?

Reality is so hard to find when you've been conditioned to
believe whatever it is you see —
let's live inside our misinterpretations forever,
just you (and you)
            and me (and me).

Small Town Savior

I love you as I once loved myself,
but better.

I miss you as though you are
part of me –
as though you are the piece
of myself that is good,
the part of me that deserves missing.

I told myself I wouldn't
love someone like this again
but I have told better,
more believable lies.

Put on whatever makes you
feel prettiest and meet me
in the yard tonight.

Make-Believe

The weight of you here, with me.
The songbird sings me to sleep
and I wake beneath your gaze.
Sweet surrender and a chapped-lipped kiss.
Gold for you though you
prefer silver, oh you
shiver when the moonlight hits.
Emotionally bruised baby and our angel with a fist,
the forest sways with our breath.
Do we dare? you ask, but the answer is always yes.

Look at me with your streetlight eyes —
green and yellow, mouth red.
We don't belong here but we make it home anyway,
settle into the sheets beneath the rising sun.
Loose-lipped lover, you never know what to say
so you say everything all at once and
leave me with the responsibility of silence.

Sit with me, please.
Pretend. Pretend.

A Poem for the Only Soul I Know in Connecticut

I miss the things I thought I hated
like your smoking,
electronic or otherwise.
I miss opinions I once detested
and our constant arguments outside
the buildings we used to shift like spirits beside.
We were two stubborn souls on an
uncomfortable park bench,
fighting the moon down.

I sit here and think of our friendship over breakfast,
living in the past until the cereal runs out.

Again

I want you
and – oh, –
I crave you too.

I crave your teeth
on my skin
as you tell me
to begin,
to lose my inhibitions
and let you feast.

Do you know
just what it is
you've started?

Have you loved
a woman like me
yet?

I welcome second chances
if in them there's the promise
I'll get hurt again.

What I Have in Common
with the Garden

Ivy grows through the stones
and the rain that caresses the petals
bounces off the thorns, unharmed.

Here is proof that maybe there is
beauty enough in rough,
immovable things.

Here comes my prayer,
my most selfish wish —
that perhaps you could
grow to love me exactly as I am.

Quarter Century

Is it too late to be happy?
I watch as the world crumbles
and remember it as I once saw it –
as something beautiful.

When we are children,
we believe that because
something is unknown,
it is better.

How many nights did I dream
of days like these – no longer
eighteen – my unwanted adolescent years
behind me?

There are new lines beneath
my eyes; I read them
the same way some read palms.
They tell me stories of the woman
I will be, whisper memories of the girl
I was but outgrew.

These days I feel like I could hold
all of the love I have left in
one closed fist. None of the things I
taught myself to believe exist inside me,
not now.

So I sit on the concrete and offer
what is left of me to the sun, the earth.
These are the things that make sense to me.
Here, in the city, these elements will outlive me.

A cloud covers the sun and I watch the rain
roll in and I become some small miracle. I am a
stunted saint, a god with bills to pay,
a woman who has begun to age.

The rain falls and I wash away.

Darreon at Dawn

Sun-baked linen, cotton-spun sheets
you roll over in your sleep to face me.
I touch your dark brow, smooth it
beneath my pink fingertips.
You are afraid, but you have
no reason to be.
Here, in bed, I understand all of humanity.

I would protect you, would protect
the house we live in,
with everything that I am,
with everything I have.
I tell you, a whisper in your ear —
a just past six secret —
that I would fight for you.

Whatever that means.

A Letter I'll Leave Beneath the Doorframe of Your Heart

Here, sit and rest.
The bones in our legs crack as
we bend our knobby knees.
I have known you
in spring, have loved you
through each of the seasons, I think.

Who would've thought? you say
and you smell like coffee and the
laundry soap we both use.
We made it, I say, and we watch the
rain fall onto the grass, the window
beginning to fog from the heater.

Every day can feel like a victory
when you know you have something
that you will one day lose
so I hold you a little tighter,
close my arms around you.

Her Last Breath

If this is it
ring the bell,
turn on the sirens
and send me off
with a salute –
military-made,
time served in
a bathroom stall
learning how to
breathe again –
where do we go?
Nowhere,
Everywhere.
Turn out the light
run the stop sign
and take me home.
Take me home.

Sequel

Should I escape?
Should I run?
The waves are rougher now,
splashing sand upon my calves
where I stand.

The thoughts inside my head
are evil things, she said,
I didn't believe in God
until I met the devil instead.

Laguna

You love to be mine, don't you?
Your fingers are folded beside my own.

It's so easy, isn't it?
Don't leave, don't leave.
Turn on the stove and let's eat.

We can waste the rest of the night away
and go to sleep with our knees pressed together.
Dream, dream, dream.

You sleep with your mouth open like I do.
If someone were to creep inside our room
while we were asleep,
all they would hear would be the sound of
us breathing from our open mouths, teeth shining in
the dark with remnants of the same toothpaste
at the corners of our lips.

This is everything I ever wanted.
No, let me say it better. You are.

Know Me, Know Me

Blurry-eyed baby
look at me and
sigh with something
akin to relief, a better cousin,
a breath escaping your lips
with purpose beyond survival.

Touch me and tell me
without speaking
how much you care for me.
Feel the ridges of me,
poetry for the blind,
and know the skin you
touch is as well as your own.

You live inside my mind,
sleeping among half-spent stars.
You are the brightest thing for miles
in that resolute darkness —
the sun sets on your shoulders
as you grab my hand and
take me.

Wanderer

Oxygen-starved lungs and
a habit for it —
living for the moment just before
the lights turn back on
when you think,
if just for a moment,
that maybe God lived in
your childhood bedroom
and got lost
on the way home.

Apocalypse Angel

When it all fades away,
what will be left of us
my dear?

Where do we go
after the wedding dress rots
and the house crumbles into
a mound of memories?

Where will we be watching from,
thousands of years from now,
when we watch the world burn?

Wherever we are, will you hold me
as the flames burn up the brush
where there was once an ocean?

Can you kiss my temple
to calm me down
when the stars fall?

It's the end of the world,
they'll say, and we'll tell them
it always feels that way, doesn't it?

Then we'll fold them into
our phantom arms and
carry them to wherever we'll be
coming from.

My Spirit

I saw myself as a ghost last night.
I looked out of my dirty window
through the blinds and
there I was — there I was.

She was watching me,
the light of the fireplace
reflecting through the window
across the grass, crackling softly
like the thunderclouds in
the summer-starved winter sky.

There was an emotion I couldn't recognize
in her eyes — it was then that I realized
I was looking at a version of myself
that did not have you in her life.

For if I died without you, it would
not be myself I would haunt. No,
I would crawl from my grave and
haunt you until you saw me,
until you took what was right
in front of you.

In your flesh, in your warm hands
I would materialize and our
souls would start to dance.

You could never get rid of me
but you would never want to.

The ghost stirs from where she stands.
There is no room for her here,
but I watch her leave anyway,
wishing her a path that leads to
some other version of you.

Crying in a Target Parking Lot

Because I miss you
and I sent you a text
but it was marked not delivered.

It hit me like a kiss that
you're not getting over this
and the grave with your name
is real and it's the same thing
I've always feared –

I think I'm disappearing
because you aren't here
to perceive me.

Thinking Small

Have you forgotten what is meant to exist
in a body that hadn't yet stopped growing taller?
It's often I look behind my shoulder to see myself
at seven. How angry I was! And how lonely that anger felt
— like I was carrying stones in all the pockets meant to carry
daisies.

I suppose we all must feel like some small part of us
is still sitting on the corner of a twin bed somewhere,
waiting for something to swoop in and save us. Oh, if they
could not have saved us, perhaps at least they would have
understood. I still remember that being a child felt like
knowing the definition of something before the word.

An Ode to Empty Pages

The beginning of something, again,
written in pencil instead of pen
because if there is one thing I have
learned about myself it is that
I will err – I will ruin what is good
if it means I will make something
of it at the end.

When I first found it,
I'd thought to cradle it –
nurture my pen as if it were
a child before I pressed it to the page.
Now it is a dog – no, something
else – a fly perhaps, buzzing against
a shut window until I get up
to let it out.

Writing is not a chore. Instead,
it is like a scab at my ankle
I scratch in my sleep
only to wake to blood at the foot
of my sheets – something I can't
help but do even if it causes a cessation
of my own healing.

Here, I say as I hold my heart in my hands.
Like this, I am a pagan of old, void of an understanding
anything but what is in front of me.

Read this and tell me what you think, please.

Fin.

Acknowledgements

Though so many souls aided in the creation of this collection, I would like to first thank my parents. Without you, I would not have had the courage to pursue writing, for it was you who first acknowledged me as something of a writer.

I would like to thank my spouse and muse, Darreon. Your love is constant and unwavering and I can only hope to capture a fraction of the joy and light you bring me in my work. Though these last few years have been some of the most emotionally strenuous years we've yet to live through, you have been a refuge and a place of strength for me and I love you.

I would like to thank my siblings — my beautiful sisters Cassie and Jenna and my lovely baby brother Jayden — whose support meant the world to me at five, at fifteen, and now, at twenty-five. What a pleasure it is to be your older sister. Everything I do, I do in hopes of making you proud.

To my dear friends — if you think one of these poems is about you, it probably is. As someone who constantly doubts herself, you give me friendships I never have to worry over. I can't help but try to immortalize my favorite things about you.

I experienced a tremendous loss in 2020. I lost someone very dear to me and was unable to say goodbye. This collection is dedicated to her, my beloved Mimi, Trudie Lee. I would like to thank her for loving me so deeply that I still feel that love now. I was very much an adult when you passed, but you always loved me like I was just learning to walk. And how I loved feeling small sometimes.

To my Papa, I love you. All those years sitting in front of your deep mahogany bookshelves staring at the gold titles on the dark spines of your favorite books left me wishing I could make something that felt as concrete as a hardback mystery novel. I'm getting there!

Lastly, while I was going through one of the darkest year of my life, I stumbled upon a band called BTS. I'd written a line here before I removed it along the lines of *at the chance of sounding silly* but how silly it would be for me to diminish something that has had such an impact on my life because I was afraid of how you might perceive me. On any account, their music genuinely brought me peace and comfort and joy at a time I felt anything but those things. As a writer, I deeply admire their songwriting and poetry and their music has most definitely inspired some of the pieces in this collection. So, to them and to all the wonderful friends I've made since because of them, thank you very much.

To anyone reading this, I sincerely hope you enjoyed this collection. Please know that you are loved.

Index

Part 1.
HISTORY

Part 2.
MODERNITY

About the Author

Poet Natalie Ann was born and raised in Southern California, where she still currently resides with her husband and their dog. Her first poetry collection, *Hands like Oceans,* explores themes such as young love alongside the California coastline.

You can find her on Instagram as @bynatalieann